Inside the
Cricket's Burrow

by Dawn Bluemel Oldfield

Consultants:

J. Howard Frank, DPhil
Entomology and Nematology Department, University of Florida

Kimberly Brenneman, PhD
National Institute for Early Education Research, Rutgers University, New Brunswick, New Jersey

BEARPORT
PUBLISHING

New York, New York

Credits
Cover, © Albert Visage/FLPA; 2–3, © Piotr Naskrecki/FLPA; 4–5, © Thinkstock and © Fabio Pupin/FLPA; 7TL, © Florian Andronache/Shutterstock; 7TR, © Sergey Dubrov/Shutterstock; 7B, © Marcel Jancovic/Shutterstock; 8, © Grimplet/Shutterstock; 9, © Pascal Goetgheluck/Ardea; 10, © Daniel Heuclin/NHPA/Photoshot; 11, © Albert Visage/FLPA; 12T, © PHOTO FUN/Shutterstock; 12C, © Henrik Larsson/Shutterstock; 12B, © schankz/Shutterstock; 13, © Pascal Goetgheluck/Ardea; 14, © Reinhard Hölzl/Imagebroker/FLPA; 15, © John Watkins/FLPA; 16, © Fabio Pupin/FLPA; 17, © Paul Choate, Entomology & Nematology Dept., University of Florida; 18, © Lyle Buss, Entomology & Nematology Dept., University of Florida; 19, © Stanislav Shinkarenko; 20, © Lyle Buss, Entomology & Nematology Dept., University of Florida; 21, © D. Kucharski K. Kucharska/Shutterstock; 22, 23TL, © Albert Visage/FLPA; 23TR, © Sergey Dubrov/Shutterstock; 23BL, © skynetphoto/Shutterstock and © Panachai Cherdchucheep/Shutterstock; 23BR, © Lyle Buss, Entomology & Nematology Dept., University of Florida.

Publisher: Kenn Goin
Senior Editor: Joyce Tavolacci
Creative Director: Spencer Brinker
Design: Emma Randall
Photo Researcher: Ruby Tuesday Books Ltd

Library of Congress Cataloging-in-Publication Data

Bluemel Oldfield, Dawn.
   Inside the cricket's burrow / by Dawn Bluemel Oldfield.
      p. cm. — (Snug as a bug: where bugs live)
   Includes bibliographical references and index.
   ISBN-13: 978-1-61772-906-5 (library binding) — ISBN-10: 1-61772-906-X (library binding)
   1. Crickets—Juvenile literature. 2. Crickets—Habitations—Juvenile literature. I. Title.
   QL508.G8B58 2014
   595.7'26—dc23
                                        2013004335

For more information, write to Bearport Publishing Company, Inc., 45 West 21st Street, Suite 3B, New York, New York 10010. Printed in the United States of America.

10 9 8 7 6 5 4 3 2 1

Contents

Hole for a Home

It's a warm summer evening in a grassy field.

As the sun sets, a chirping **insect** crawls out of a hole in the soil.

It's a mole cricket leaving its **burrow**.

The hole is the entrance to the creature's underground home.

burrow

mole cricket

Adult mole crickets are one to two inches (2.5 to 5 cm) long and are mainly active at night.

What is a Mole Cricket?

Mole crickets are long insects that spend most of their life underground.

They live in burrows that they dig in fields, lawns, and other grassy areas.

In the United States, there are ten different kinds of mole crickets.

More than 100 different kinds live around the world.

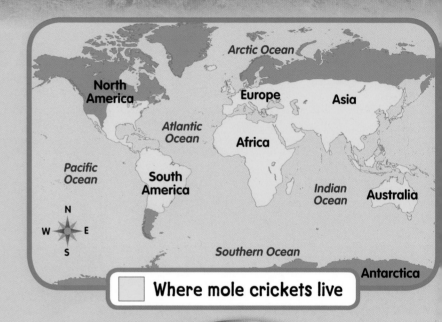

Arctic Ocean

North America

Europe

Asia

Atlantic Ocean

Africa

Pacific Ocean

South America

Indian Ocean

Australia

N
W E
S

Southern Ocean

Antarctica

Where mole crickets live

There are thousands of species, or kinds, of crickets in the world. Some live underground like mole crickets but most live above ground.

field cricket

bush cricket

mole cricket

Look at the pictures above. In what ways do the crickets look alike? In what ways do they look different?

Built for Digging

Adult mole crickets have four wings and helmet-shaped heads.

Their long, brown bodies are covered with short, silky hairs.

These hairs keep soil from sticking to their bodies as they dig.

Mole crickets have digging claws on their front legs.

Their shovel-like legs help them tunnel through the soil.

mole

Mole crickets got their name because they look like small animals called moles that also dig burrows.

digging claws

hairs

Underground Tunnels

A mole cricket begins building its burrow by digging a hole in the ground.

It uses its strong front legs to scoop up dirt and push it aside.

Then it makes short, shallow tunnels called galleries just below the ground.

The cricket also digs deeper tunnels.

Some of the tunnels lead to an escape hole, in case the insect needs to flee.

mole cricket digging

The hole leading to a mole cricket's burrow is about a half inch around (1.3 cm). That's about the size of a dime.

gallery

Why do you think mole crickets dig both shallow and deep tunnels?

Favorite Foods

During the day, mole crickets hide inside their deep tunnels.

At night, however, they move closer to the surface to feed.

They crawl in the shallow galleries to search for a meal.

Roots and plant stems are some of their favorite foods.

They also munch on small insects and earthworms.

Mole Cricket Foods

fire ants

rove beetle

earthworm

Staying Safe

Mole crickets need to be careful.

Birds, rats, skunks, and insects hunt and eat them.

Luckily, mole crickets have ways to stay safe from their enemies.

The crickets' brown color helps them blend in with the soil and stay hidden.

They also stay safe by hiding in the deep tunnels of their burrows.

mole cricket blending in with the soil

If a mole cricket is attacked inside its burrow, it can use an escape hole to get away.

mole cricket

Sometimes mole crickets leave their burrows to find food or escape from an enemy. Why else might a mole cricket leave its burrow?

15

Singing for a Mate

During the spring, male and female mole crickets come together to **mate**.

To attract a female, the male rubs its wings together.

The rubbing makes long, fast buzzing sounds called trills: *"Trrrrrrrrrrrrrrr. Trrrrrrrrrrrrrrr."*

Some kinds of male mole crickets trill at the openings of their burrows.

Others trill in special horn-shaped burrows that they dig.

male at opening to burrow

horn-shaped burrow

male mole cricket

gallery

tunnel

tunnel to escape hole

The unusual trumpet shape of the burrow makes the male's trills sound even louder.

Mole Cricket Mother

Once a female hears the trills, she flies to the male's burrow to mate.

After mating, the female digs a round room in the male's burrow.

She lays her eggs there, each of which is covered with a sticky liquid.

Some females stay close to the burrow to care for their eggs.

mole cricket eggs

Some experts think that the sticky liquid made by mother mole crickets helps protect the eggs from disease.

mother mole cricket

eggs

Growing Up

After three to four weeks, the eggs hatch.

The baby mole crickets are called **nymphs**.

The nymphs are much smaller than their parents and have no wings.

After three to four months, the hatchlings reach their adult size and grow wings.

Soon the young mole crickets will be digging their own burrows—and trilling their own songs!

mole cricket nymphs

Newly hatched nymphs are about a quarter of an inch (0.6 cm) in length. That's about the size of a grain of rice!

adult mole cricket

Science Lab

Be A Mole Cricket Scientist

Imagine that you are a scientist who studies mole crickets. Write a report to tell people all about the mole cricket and its burrow. Draw pictures to include in your report. Use the photos and information in this book to help you.

When you are finished, present your report to your friends and family.

Here are some words that you can use when writing or talking about the mole cricket and its burrow.

tunnels	mate	entrance hole	stays safe
burrow	shovel-like legs	trilling	galleries

Read the questions below and think about the answers. You can include some of the information from your answers in your report and drawings.

- *How does a mole cricket build its home? What body parts does it use?*

- *Why are the tunnels in a mole cricket's burrow important?*

- *How does a male mole cricket find a mate?*

- *Where does a mother mole cricket keep her eggs?*

Science Words

burrow (BUR-oh) a hole or tunnel built by an insect, spider, or other animal to live in

insect (IN-sekt) a small animal that has six legs, three main body parts, two antennas, and a hard outer covering

mate (MAYT) to come together in order to have young

nymphs (NIMFS) young insects that change into adults by growing and shedding their hard outer covering

Index

Read More

Bodden, Valerie. *Crickets (Creepy Creatures).* Mankato, MN: Creative Education (2011).

Gonzales, Doreen. *Crickets in the Dark (Creatures of the Night).* New York: PowerKids Press (2010).

Miller, Sara Swan. *Grasshoppers and Crickets of North America (Animals in Order).* New York: Franklin Watts (2002).

Learn More Online

To learn more about crickets and their burrows, visit **www.bearportpublishing.com/SnugasaBug**

About the Author

Dawn Bluemel Oldfield is a freelance writer. When she isn't writing, she enjoys reading, traveling, and working in her garden. She and her husband live in Prosper, Texas, where crickets often chirp at night.